PROCAFFEINATING: (n) the tendency to not start anything until you've had a cup of coffee.

COFFEE
TEXTBOOK

Edgars Kazlausks

Journey Bean to Cup

No matter where you are or how you like your cup: the phrase "Let's get a cup of coffee" just never gets old. Coffee cuts through ages and cultures, bedtimes and hangovers. What many people don't realise is that the same beverage that wakes you up, gets you through the day or ends your dinner, is the product of a long journey and the hard work of many people!
Moreover, the days when a cup of coffee was just a coffee are long gone. It can be quite confusing looking at a coffee menu nowadays! There are so many options now that it may be hard to make a good choice without some inside information of what is what.

This is why I decided to share some of my thoughts on the topic. I've worked in the coffee industry for many years exploring different coffee shops and coffee roastery approaches to the product of coffee. During this time, I've taken countless courses, I've conferred with coffee enthusiasts, and I've served and tasted thousands of cups. I'd like to take mine and my colleagues experience and give you a comprehensive introduction to coffee as we know it today. I have experimented not only with the brewing process but also the roasting process to find the potential of each coffee bean and the ways to highlight it's best characteristics. My work has been driven by customer feedback. Analysing customers preferences and understanding what coffee means to them has allowed me to better meet their requirements while introducing them to new ideas and flavours, in order to show them what coffee has to offer. I am not claiming to know everything about coffee, nor do I want to imply that there is not only one way that things should be done.

This book is the result of many facts I've gleaned from the business over the years, topped up with quotes from other coffee professionals and the research of several companies who are participating in this project in order to spread the word about coffee. So... make your order or brew a fresh cup... and allow me to introduce you to coffee.

• Coffee is actually a seed, not a bean, (But let's avoid revolt and just stick to the term in usage, which is bean)
• Coffee can be an exciting adventure for your taste buds.
• Coffee can be a hobby.
Coffee can be a full time job.
• Coffee can be the passion of a lifetime.
• Coffee can be more than just a biter fix of caffeine.

When you acknowledge coffee flavour characteristics and understand how one variety of coffee differs from another, you can have different experiences. Coffee stops being "just a coffee" and turns into something more exciting! By making yourself aware of the distinct qualities that your coffee has, alongside that much-needed morning caffeine kick, you might wonder... 'What makes coffee taste like this?' 'Why does it taste so good in cafes?' As in cooking and other crafts, only two things truly matter. These are
• The quality of the product itself and
• The way that it is made.

By experimenting, roasters have found ways to show off the best characteristics of a complex product. Finding differences in taste from origin to origin and understanding how different techniques in preparation affect a cup make coffee all the more intriguing. But what motivates coffee makers more than anything else these days is the pursuit of perfection. This pursuit pushes boundaries, so that coffee develops and improves every day!

"There is nothing in this world that you can't turn into heroin."
                                        -Get Him to the Greek, 2010

If a coffee bean is a seed... is there a fruit? The answer is yes. The seed is found inside of the fruit, which is called a cherry. The "Dancing goats" legend describes how the first coffee plant was discovered by a goatherd named Kaldi in Ethiopia.

Kaldi noticed that goats eating cherries from a certain bush became more active. After trying the berries himself, he brought them to the monks nearby. However the monks disapproved of them for their mood-enhancing properties and threw the berries into a fire. Thus, the first coffee beans were roasted. The monks couldn't resist the aroma of the seeds on the fire and decided to give mood-enhancing another chance. This time, they ground and dissolved the beans in hot water, thus brewing the first cup of coffee.

Let's have a closer look

When cutting the coffee cherry in half you can see 5 layers

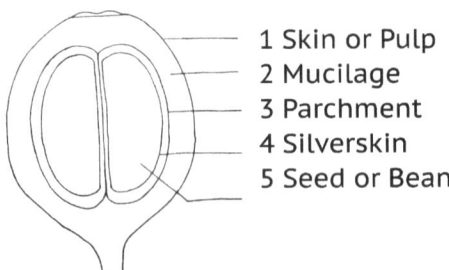

1 Skin or Pulp
2 Mucilage
3 Parchment
4 Silverskin
5 Seed or Bean

(There are usually two half beans inside one cherry with the exception of the Peaberry which contains only one round bean)

Is there only one type of coffee?

The answer is no. The coffee genus has more than 120 different species! The two most commonly used are Coffea Arabica and Coffea Canephora, which goes by the name Robusta.

Although both of these coffee species come from the same family tree, they are very different. Think of them the way you think of green and red grapes: although each is totally different in colour and taste, both are still known by the same name of grapes.

Arabica versus Robusta

The Arabica coffee bean is bigger and has a wavy line across it's body. The Robusta bean is smaller and more round in shape, with a straight line across its body.

If you are chasing caffeine, then Robusta is what you seek, because it contains nearly twice as much caffeine as Arabica. This is the reason why the Robusta plant is less sensitive to pests. Its extra caffeine acts as a defence system, because the caffeine is toxic to insects. The Robusta plant is also less vulnerable to diseases and climate change. It grows in low altitudes of 0- 800 MSL (meters above sea level)

The Arabica plant grows in altitudes from 600 -2200 MSL and is more sensitive to diseases, pests, and climate change.

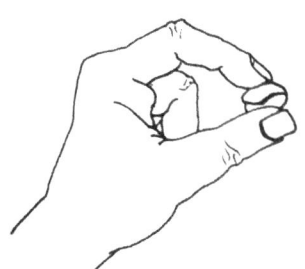

This makes the Arabica plant more difficult to farm. The Arabica plant also produces less crop than the Robusta plant. Because of this the price of Arabica coffee tends to be more expensive than that of Robusta.

Now, the taste.

Arabica has much more acidity and is lighter and sweeter than Robusta.
In comparison, Robusta tastes bitter, is lower in acidity and has a rich body (and flavour is often described as rubbery)

When made into espresso, Robusta creates more crema than the espresso Arabica.
(Crema- A golden brown layer that covers the surface of a cup of espresso)

By blending these two coffee beans together, you can create a cup that includes qualities from both beans, combining different levels of acidity, sweetness, body, bitterness and crema. Blends like these are often used in traditional cafes.

Two or more coffee beans from different origins mixed together are called blends. Coffee beans that are selected to be used in a blend are each given a flavour profile, since one might have more sweetness and another more acidity or body.

Coffee beans specifically from one country are called 'single origin'. If it is from just one region of country, the more appropriate term is 'Single estate'
For more about cup qualities, see page 13

Variables
Environmental effect on coffee flavour

Many variables, all of which have a massive impact on taste, are taken into account when sourcing coffee. A good understanding of these variables comes in handy when looking for specific flavour notes.

• The processing method of the coffee can affect its flavour. This includes how the coffee beans have been treated in order to separate them from the cherry and the way they are dried (there are wet , dry and honey processes).

• The country/continent where the coffee was grown might have certain flavour characteristics. Taking a reverse route, recognising a coffee's distinct flavours/ characteristics can help determine where the coffee is from. These different characteristics are determined by the different climates/ soils/ altitudes the coffee is grown.

• Coffee that is grown at a higher altitude typically has fruitier notes than coffee grown at a lower altitude.

• Coffee plant species differ in taste. Arabica and Robusta beans taste completely different. There are also differences within species - called varieties.

• Farms soil and surroundings around coffee plants create a variety of flavours. All farmers are interested in getting the best possible harvest, so they use compost and minerals to make the healthiest soil possible for the plant.

•Each farm tends to produce one variety of coffee. Usually in straight fields exposing the coffee plants to the sun, but occasionally the same farm might present trees alongside, providing shade. Coffee grown in the shade is called 'shade grown'.

•One of the variables that we can only hope to have in our favour is the weather. Good air temperature and rain is vital for a good harvest. If the temperature or amount of rain goes above or below the norm, it can result in a smaller harvest, meaning that the price of the coffee produced would go up.

Origins

With the help from 'Coffee Imports' (a green, coffee-importing company) I have made up a list of some of the countries that produce coffee. If this list intrigues you, I'd recommend taking a trip to one of the countries to see for yourself what happens when the cherries are ripe. I have noted the approximate period when each country harvests, so that you'll know the best time to visit. Just a warning: the harvest time can change year by year, due to differences in the weather and micro-climates of given countries. Use this list as a checklist and check off the different countries as you visit them. There are over 70 coffee growing countries, all of which are located in the tropics. They form a band across the globe that is known as the 'coffee belt'.

Country	Harvest
Angola	April - June
Australia	September - December
Benin	April - June
Bolivia	July - October
Borneo	June - December
Borneo	April - August
Brazil	May - August
Burundi	April - September
Cameroon	October - December
Central African Republic	November - March
Colombia	October - March; September - December
Costa Rica	November - March
Cuba	July - February
Dominican Republic	November - April
Ecuador	September - December

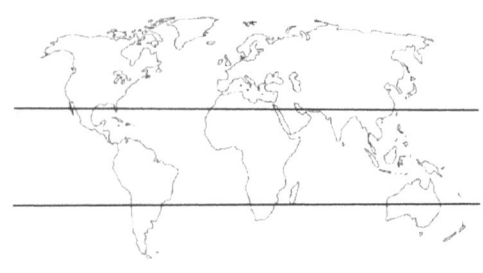

El Salvador	November - March
Haiti	August - March
Hawaii	November - March
Honduras	October - February
Ivory Coast	November - April
Jamaica	January - March
Java	June - October
Kenya	November - April
Madagascar	June - September
Malawi	December - February
Mexico	October - March
Nepal	December - March
Nicaragua	December - March
Nigeria	November - March
Panama	November - March
Papua New Guinea	May - August
Paraguay	June - September
Peru	July - September
Philippines	December - March
Puerto Rico	September - November
Republic of the Congo	September - October
Rwanda	March - July
Sierra Leone	December - February
Sri Lanka	August
Sulawesi	May - November
Sumatra	October - March
Tanzania	October - December
Thailand	October - March
Timor	June - September
Togo	November - February
Republic of Trinidad and Tobago	November - February
Uganda	October - January
Venezuela	October - January
Vietnam	December - January
Yemen	October - December
Zambia	May - July
Zimbabwe	July - October

Not to be forgotten is how the coffee beans find their way to local roasters and cafes. Not all roasters buy coffee directly from farms. Coffee import companies play a major role in sourcing coffee as well as planning the logistics of delivering the beans, so that the beans can be successfully passed down the chain on their journey into our cups. Importing companies connect sellers with buyers and help build relationships that benefit everyone.

"'Café Imports' works throughout the year to source the a wide range of specialty coffees. We are always focused on quality, but are keen to add value to the lives of producers. As such at the moment, my work and the work of my colleagues is the task for me and my colleagues is primarily in finding partnerships with interesting, quality-driven coffee producers and trying to support them as much as possible by purchasing not just the microlot coffees but also the workhorse coffees that may make up the bulk of their harvest.

Personally, I was involved in helping select the Brazilian coffees for Café Imports Europe for the year 2016/2017. It was an immense pleasure to meet and share a coffee with the producers themselves and also understand how our partners at origin are constantly trying to innovate to produce better, more sustainable and interesting coffees.

We work as hard as possible to get coffee from origin to our warehouse and ultimately to our customers as quickly as possible. A lot depends on how far away the origin country is located, but issues like trucking strikes, issues with shipping containers and regulatory barriers can seriously delay the shipment of coffee from any origin. Overall, it is likely to take 2-4 months for most coffee to go from tree to our warehouses."

Stuart Ritson
Sales Associate
cafeimportseurope.com

"I am a coffee fanatic. Once you go to proper coffee, you can't go back. You cannot go back."

-Hugh Laurie

This is the busiest time of the year for coffee farmers. When coffee cherries are ripe, they are ready to be gathered and processed. Harvesting can be completed in 3 ways.

- Selective picking is done by hand-picking the ripe cherries one at a time. This is called a 'Quality' harvesting method, as only the ripest (sweetest) cherries are selected to be harvested. However, a downside of this method is that it is very time consuming. The cherry pickers need to visit the cherry tree at several different times, as the cherries take different times to ripen. Hence, the cost of production is higher.
- Stripping is completed by hand collecting all the cherries from a branch by running a hand down each branch, gathering both ripe and unripe cherries. This is a faster method than selective picking, as all the cherries from the branch get picked at one time, so there is no need to revisit the tree after picking.
- The machine method of picking is similar to the stripping method. However, all the cherries are stripped from the branch using a machine. This method is usually used in large farms, and it speeds up the harvesting time.

After gathering the coffee cherries, the next step is processing them. There are 3 processing methods:

Dry Process

The beans are dried while still inside the cherry. The cherries are usually spread across large patios or raised beds to be dried by the sun. They are periodically mixed so that they dry evenly. After 4-6 days the volume of the berries will decrease as the fruit dries, and the moisture content of the bean drops to about 11%. This process is monitored with a moisture meter. During the next step the dried cherries are removed from the patio and into milling machines, which will separate the bean, dried cherry and the last layer called silver skin. Now the beans are ready to be sorted into sizes and graded. Typically, dry-processed natural coffees are low in acidity, full-bodied and very sweet.

Wet Process/ Washed Process

Firstly, the beans are sorted according to density in a water channel. The good cherries will sink, and the cherries that float are removed. Next the cherry skin is removed mechanically, leaving the sticky fruit part (which is called mucilage) on the beans. They are then placed in fermentation tanks for 24-36 hours until the soft fruit part loosens and can be removed completely. After this, the beans are either dried in the sun or by drying machines, until their moisture content is down to 11%. Wet-processed coffees tend to be low-bodied and high in acidity.

Pulped Natural or Honey Process

The cherry skin is removed by pulping machines. The beans, still with their mucilage layer, are then laid out to dry. There is a risk of mold, due to the sugar content in the mucilage of the beans. The beans are mixed multiple times an hour.
Honey-processed coffees have medium acidity, medium body and are very sweet. They quite often have boozy aromas.
The word "Honey" refers to the mucilage, because its sweetness and stickiness is similar to honey. The amount of mucilage remaining on the bean's surface determines the sweetness and the body of the flavour. Variations in the honey process are broken down into four subcategories:

• White Honey- all or nearly all of the mucilage is removed
• Golden Honey- 75% of the mucilage is removed
• Yellow Honey – 50% of the mucilage is removed
• Red Honey -25% of the mucilage is removed

Apart from the above commercially used processing methods (dry, wet and honey processes), some more experimental methods can be used. These experimental methods are usually engineered by coffee professionals who work together with farmers to produce small quantities of unusually processed coffees.

After processing, the coffee beans are categorised by their bean sizes and the areas/altitudes where they were grown. Later on a score is given to the quality of the cup, and that score sets the price of the bean.

The area of a single farm where a particular coffee is gathered is called a "lot." In large plantations, the taste of the coffee varies according to the area where it was grown. Shade and differing altitudes across the farm affect cherry growth, so plantations are often divided into parts. The coffee from a specific part of the plantation is given a number, which corresponds to a specific lot.

The routine of scoring coffee by taste, Cupping, is very simple. You can do it wherever you are. The only necessities needed are a kettle, bowl (a small bowl, one that holds less than 250 mL of liquid), a coffee grinder and two spoons, (soup spoons also known as cupping spoons)

There is a very specific protocol for cupping, in order to ensure that everyone prepares the coffee sample in the same way. This allows you to look at a coffee sample objectively (without possible errors made in preparation that would affect the taste). Cupping protocol can differ depending on areas, coffee roasteries and open cupping sessions for the public.

The most common cupping protocol runs as follows: a sample is prepared, using a 55g/L coffee-to-water ratio, or 10g of coffee to 180g of water. Water at a temperature of 94°-96°C is added to the coffee, in the preceding proportions, and it is brewed for 4 minutes. A crust appears on top of the coffee in the bowl, and the back of one spoon is used to break the crust, then both spoons are used to remove it. After this, the coffee is tasted with a loud slurp from one of the cupping spoons. Slurping loudly gets air into your mouth and activates the coffee flavours.

Coffee is scored and judged in the following categories:

• Clean cup - Free of defects (defects such as mouldy beans, beans damaged by insects, over fermentation, all of which can give coffee a bad taste) overpowering a coffee characteristics.
• Sweetness- sweetness of the cup
• Acidity- Brightness of the cup
• Flavour- Intensity of flavour, and characteristics of coffee.
• Aftertaste-The taste that lingers in the mouth after the coffee has been swallowed
• Mouthfeel-Tactile- texture, viscosity, also the weight and the body of the coffee (full, medium light body)
• Overall- This is a personal opinion. Was the cup average or extraordinary?

These seven categories yield a maximum score of 100 points.
Coffee that scores up to 60 points is graded as "commercial" coffee.
Coffee with a score between 60-80 points is considered "good."
Coffee scoring 80-100 points is known as "specialty grade" coffee.

I would not necessarily say that everyone should feel the need to go out on a limb for those 80+ point coffee bags, or chase very rare and limited coffees. They are very expensive and you might not like them.
I have fallen in love with some, and I would very much like to encourage you to explore and find the coffee that is best suited to you by tasting a variety of different types and sorts!

"Tasting coffee is like listening to music, when everything is in balance its like a symphony, and by listening closely, can differ each instrument as each quality of coffee."

–Luke Wilson

"As green buyer for North Star Coffee Roasters, a company focused on specialty grade coffee, my first priority when choosing a coffee is its complexity of flavour, consistency and cleanliness. The desired flavour profile is completely dependent on the requirement – for instance, is the coffee going to be used as a blend component or a single origin filter? We always take into account the customer's preference and ensure that our range of coffees is seasonal but broad, guaranteeing that we have a coffee that hits most flavour profiles all year round.

A great blending coffee for me will have fantastic body and excellent sweetness with good character but a more rounded acidity, something that is not going to clash with other components. Our house blend is therefore closer to a more traditional interpretation of an espresso blend and is made up of coffees from Brazil, El Salvador and Sumatra to produce a full bodied, rich and chocolatey blend with good sweetness and low acidity so that it is great as espresso or as a milk based drink.

The single origin filter category is by far my favourite as it is so broad and gives me real opportunity to source a wide range of coffees that have really distinct flavour notes as these will come through using this type of brew method. It is our chance to have a bit of fun with the coffees that we source as we are less restricted – a washed Kenyan with intense and pointed acidity for instance is really difficult to work with and show off through the espresso machine; put it through a Chemex or V60 Pour over though and you will be able to pinpoint those incredible flavours of blackcurrant, butter and lemon. For this category, I tend to cup for complexity over anything else and will automatically go for the coffees that taste the least like coffee! A natural processed Ethiopian with jammy notes of blueberry and mango or a fresh crop washed Colombian with pointed lemon acidity and flavours of peach and butter will win every time!

Since our inception in 2013, we have always had an intense focus on quality control.

Cupping, roast analysis and experimenting with brewing have been second nature to us from the start due to my background in green coffee whilst working for a coffee importer company. Our quality control procedures are the backbone of our business and not only safeguard us against any batch queries but also help us to continually amend and improve what we are doing.

We cup all of our production roasts from the day before each morning and use a roast colour meter to analyse our consistency. This allows us an insight into how a green coffee is developing or ageing and directs our roast profile adjustments – it can also dictate when we remove a coffee from our offer list. We also test all espresso blends weekly and use a VST refractometer when creating blends to ensure we are producing coffees that taste great and are easy to work with.

Our dedication to quality control has resulted in the establishment of our Coffee Academy through which we offer the SCAE Sensory Skills modules – we have had a number of industry professionals, including other roasters and importers, come through our doors to learn about SCAA cupping standards and the implementation of quality control in the workplace. We cannot emphasise enough the importance of a stringent quality control procedure – no matter the size of your business, you should always have an insight into what you are producing and be able to pinpoint any issues back through the supply chain to encourage a positive cycle of experimentation and quality improvement.

Most of my favourite coffees would tend to be East African (Kenyan/Ethiopian/Rwandan) due to the high levels of acidity and intensity of flavour, but I can also find these characteristics in a high grown Colombian – as a coffee producing origin, Colombia possibly holds the most interest for me due to its potential for flavour experimentation as a result of the huge variance in growing regions. My preferred brew method is the Chemex so by default I tend to gravitate towards washed coffees with excellent cleanliness and complexity."

Holly Bowman
Green coffee buyer
www.northstarroast.com

Certifications

Coffee farm certifications, like for any other type of farm, show that the farm is meeting a certain standard. The type of certification can also ensure that when the coffee is bought, the money from the purchase goes to helping the region of the farm.

However, opinions around coffee certifications is divided. Does the money really go to the people working the farm or not? Should you choose to by a certified product or not? It is, entirely your choice! To help you decide, here are the most common certifications and their purposes.

 UTZ stands for sustainable farming with better opportunities for farmers, their families and our planet. UTZ aims to create a world where sustainable farming is the norm;

where farmers implement good agricultural practices and manage their farms profitably with respect for people and planet, industry invests in and rewards sustainable production and consumers can enjoy and trust the products they buy.

 Rainforest Alliance – Created in the 1980's. The Rainforest Alliance is an international non-profit organisation that works to conserve biodiversity and ensure sustainable livelihoods.

Products bearing the Rainforest Alliance Certified™ seal contain ingredients that were produced on farms that are required to meet comprehensive standards for sustainable agriculture to help protect the environment and the rights and welfare of workers, their families and communities.

Bird Friendly®" is a certification that accompanies organic certification, identifying coffee farms with a shade tree canopy that mimics the forest-like habitat that birds require-especially migratory songbirds.

The Bird Friendly (BF) seal assures consumers that the coffee they drink comes from a farm that has been inspected and certified by a third party as viable, quality habitat for birds. BF farmers are helping to provide this habitat and are rewarded with a price premium for their management practices. More information can be obtained at the Smithsonian Migratory Bird Center's website (si.edu/smbc). BF links conservation to the market place.

Fairtrade is about better prices, decent working conditions and fair terms of trade for farmers and workers. It's about supporting the development of thriving farming and worker communities.

The Mark means that the Fairtrade ingredients in the product have been produced by small-scale farmer organisations or plantations that meet Fairtrade social, economic and environmental standards. The standards include protection of workers' rights and the environment, payment of the Fairtrade Minimum Price and an additional Fairtrade Premium to invest in business or community projects.

Coffee Roasting

Coffee roasting is similar to baking. All you do is drop green coffee beans into a preheated coffee roaster and let them rotate around for up to 20 minutes. In this time the entire chemical structure of the coffee bean changes; this is evidenced when the colour changes from green to yellow to orange to brown as the bean expands in size.

The roaster can alter the way coffee beans change in taste by altering the length of the roast cycle, the temperature, or other parameters that affect the progression of the roast. This is known as the roast profile and acts as a recipe for the roast.

Different coffee beans call for different roast profiles. Nothing is consistent or certain when working with coffee, so quality control (cupping) is a huge part of a roast masters work. It is important to monitor the process, so that there are no roast defects and to make changes if necessary in order to meet the expected standards.

As you look at a roasted coffee bean, the first thing you will notice is its appearance and colour, particularly how dark the bean is (the roast degree). Green beans or other visible roasting defects will have a noticeable effect on quality without requiring cupping.

Roast degrees are divided into the following sections:
• Light Roast - Cinnamon
• Medium Roast -City   - Full City -Vienna
• Dark Roast -Italian/ French Roast

In lighter roasts (the bean colour is paler), the bean is more acidic and lighter in body. It is usually fruity with less of a presence of bitterness.
In darker roasts (dark bean colour), the bean has a lower acidity and more body. It will also typically have some chocolate, caramel or nut flavours.

Buying your bag of goods

At this point in our journey from bean to cup, you might have some questions before purchasing your bag of coffee beans. However, some coffee pouches speak for themselves. All the important factors we have studied that impact taste can be identified on the label of the bag; identifying factors named on most coffee bags include the roasteries name, a flavour description and the date of roast.

*Suitable for: Some coffee roasters might suggest a brewing method such as filter or espresso (which indicate the most suitable way to brew the coffee).

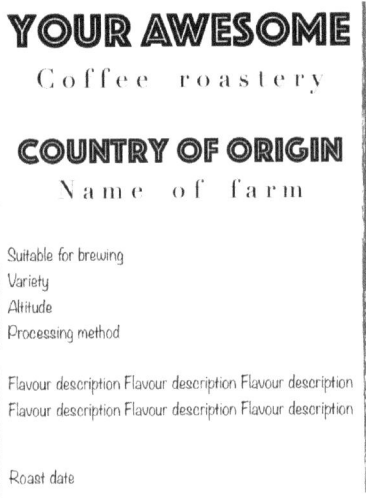

YOUR AWESOME

Coffee roastery

COUNTRY OF ORIGIN

Name of farm

Suitable for brewing
Variety
Altitude
Processing method

Flavour description Flavour description Flavour description
Flavour description Flavour description Flavour description

Roast date

Storage

Storing coffee beans properly slows the process by which the beans go stale, keeping them flavourful for longer.

It is easy to keep beans safe from damaging outside factors! Simply store in a dark, dry place in an airtight package, and the job is done. This prevents the main threats (moisture and oxygen) from getting to the coffee. Oxidation causes the coffee beans to give up their aromas and therefore go stale; airtight containers slow down this process as less oxygen can get to the beans, increasing their shelf life considerably. Freezing the coffee beans works because the low temperatures slow down oxidation. However, a risk of freezing is the damage caused by moisture due to the condensation formed by temperature changes.

How a coffee bean is ground is very important to its brew. It's advised not only to grind the coffee just before brewing, but also to pay attention to the grind size as well.

When a coffee bean is ground, its surface area is increased, so it is more soluble and can dissolve faster. However, the increased solubility makes it give off more aroma, so the ground coffee becomes stale at a faster rate than the whole bean. The surface area created by the size of the grind can change the taste of the brew massively. Whether the coffee grounds are even in size can also affect the extraction of flavour. If coffee grounds are not evenly ground, the smaller particles will give up their aroma faster than larger particles; this creates an uneven extraction (see pages 27 and 28).

Grinders

A blade grinder-

Chops and smashes the coffee beans into smaller particles. The longer the grinder runs, the smaller/ finer the particles are. This method does not really work well if you are aiming for perfection in your brew, because it is difficult to keep the size of the particles consistent. Coffee that has not been ground too finely will work for all brewing methods. But for better tasting coffee it is better to use different grind settings that match the different methods of brewing. Blade grinders do not modulate between grind sizes.

A Burr grinder-

When using a burr grinder you can change how coarse or fine the coffee beans will be ground. Burr grinders use two rings of round burrs to grind beans. Changing the distance between the two burrs changes the size of the grind. Because of this grind setting, and consistency of the coffee particles this makes a burr grinder more suitable for coffee brewing.

Burrs can be cylindrical or conical. Both of these kinds/ shapes work in the same way. The shape of the burr has no impact on the taste of the coffee produced.

Grind chart

Choosing the right grind when buying pre-ground coffee is crucial to a good tasting brew. Furthermore, I recommend choosing whole beans and grinding them just before brewing for an even better brew! See page 31 for the disadvantages of storing ground coffee.

Here are some guidelines for matching the size of ground coffee particles to different brewing methods. If you own a coffee grinder, it probably has a dial with different grinds marked on it from fine to coarse. (The norm is left for coarse and right for fine).

Quick tip: The more time that the brew method requires, the coarser the grind setting required.
(Chemex 4-7 mins = Coarse grind, Espresso 20-40 secs = Fine grind)

Fine ground suitable for: Espresso machine and Moka.
Followed by Aeropress

Medium ground - single serve 'v' Shape filer, Flat bottom Filter,

Coarse ground- Chemex, French press, multiple cup filter brewer, Cold brew

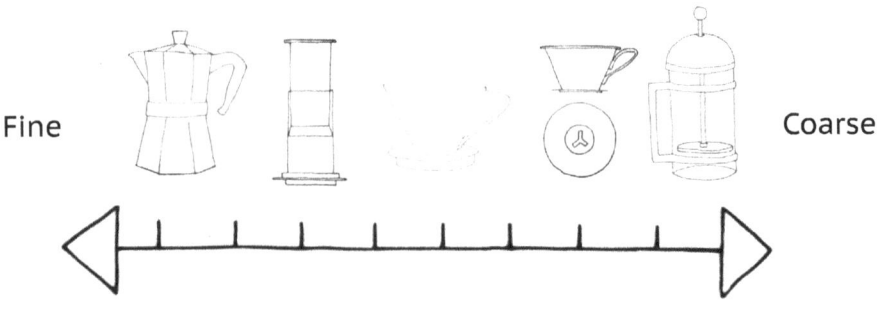

Fine   Coarse

Let's Brew!

In the next few pages we will look at some brewing methods that anyone and everyone can use at home. All you need for a perfect brew is a a kettle, grinder, scale, brewing appliance, and some awesome coffee beans!

Brewing coffee is no different from cooking anything else. There is a recipe that explains how to get the best out of your coffee beans while having a great time tasting and sharing your brew!

It's only a combination of water and coffee. If both of these are good, then the only thing (apart from brewing toys) that can make your coffee better is a bit of skill. The most important factors in brewing are as follows: Water, Brew recipe, Extraction.

Your chosen brew method is just a tool that combines two elements together, coffee and water. The method doesn't really matter, but some coffees might be more suitable (or tastier) if you use certain methods. Recommendations about brew methods such as "Espresso," "Filter," or "Aeropress" might be on the package .

The place where you buy your coffee beans should be able to advise you on the brewing method that they think is best.
Keep in mind that this is only the way that one place thinks is best. It is okay if you want to use a different method or approach. Share or guard your recipe as you like.

Home brewers fall into two categories:
•Filter/ Pour over / drip
Chemex, v60, kalita etc (any method where water falls through ground coffee (page 33, 37, 39)

•Infusion method
French Press or Caffetiere (method where water is in still contact with ground coffee)   (pages 41-44)

Different approach?
How can you do that?

Can you remember the three main factors that affect brewing results? They are water, brew recipe and extraction.
Changing the water temperature by just a few degrees can have an impact on the brew. It alters the extraction of flavour!
If an espresso runs for 10 seconds longer than its usual 25-second run time, the flavour notes of the coffee will change. (For more information on extraction, see page 27-28).

The smallest changes in a recipe can play a big role in extraction, and it can affect some coffee types more than others. On the other hand, noticing these differences is up to our sensory skills, and how well we perceive flavours and their intensity.

A brewing recipe is made of the following elements:
• Dose/Amount of coffee
• Brew ratio (the ratio of water to ground coffee, in grams)
• Extraction time
• Water temperature

"I make a mean cup of coffee, if you give me the right ingredients."
-Ice Cube

Water and its temperature

Good quality water is important in coffee brewing. Tainted water is noticeable in the brew.
Hard water - coffee lacks acidity, clarity, sweetness. Flavour can be very bitter and plain.
Soft water – coffee is very acidic, with a harsh taste.

Chemical compounds in water change the way the coffee is extracted, which brings us to the conclusion that brewed coffee tastes different depending on the source of the water (bottled water or tap water, etc.).

The ideal water temperature for brewing coffee is between 92-96C. A thermometer would be useful for this. If you don't have a thermometer handy, switch the kettle off just before the water boils, or once it boils, let it cool for a few minutes, so that it is in the right temperature range

Ratio

I suggest a ratio of 50-70g of ground coffee to 1 litre of water. This can be broken down into 25-35g of ground coffee to 500ml/g water.
Or 12.5-17.5g of ground coffee to 250ml/g water.
To maintain this coffee ratio, scales are needed to weigh the coffee grounds and the amount of water being poured on the grounds.

Time
(Time of extraction)

Each brewing method has its own optimum brewing period. This is the amount of time that it takes for the brew to bring out the best in the coffee beans. This period of time changes depending on the amount of coffee being brewed and the method of extraction.

For the infusion method (French Press), the time of extraction can be increased by letting the coffee remain in contact with the water for longer.

For filter methods, the time of extraction can be increased by using a finer grind of coffee or by pouring the water in a slower and more gentle manner. For a faster brew, a coarser grind is used with an even pouring style to ensure all the grounds are moistened.

The period of extraction is the length of time that the water is in contact with the coffee grounds. Or it can also be the time that it takes for all the water to pass through the ground coffee whilst brewing.

The time of extraction (time where water is in contact with coffee) is used as a guideline to determine the setting of the grind.

Example:
Filter method.

If your recipe states that 200g of water is supposed to pass through the coffee grounds in 2 min but it actually takes three minutes, a coarser grind is needed.

The opposite change in grinder setting is made if the coffee passes through in less than 2 min, which requires a finer grind.
A change in the setting of the grind requires a change in the period of extraction.

The goal for the right extraction is a sweet spot (normally between 18 and 22%) when the coffee tastes its best, its sweetest, and its most balanced, not overly acidic or bitter.

The more that is extracted from the coffee beans, which happens by lengthening the extraction period, the more bitter the coffee gets. If the extraction percentage is very low, then the coffee can taste very acidic and salty.

A coffee refractometer is used to find out the exact extraction percentage. It sends a light through the brewed coffee samples and measures its refraction (the angles that the light breaks into as it hits the coffee). The refractometer tells us how much extracted coffee mass is in the water. The coffee mass is used to calculate the extraction percentage.
Tools like coffee refractometers are used in many cafes/ roasteries that aim for perfection and for optimum use of the coffee beans.

There are many classes available with guided tastings to deepen your understanding of brewing, extraction levels, and the difference between under-extracted and over-extracted coffee. There are also classes in general sensory skills, which are very helpful in improving your perception, so that you learn more about what you are tasting.
See page 16, 68, for what trainers have to say about coffee courses.

Blooming

Coffee blooming is a gentle pre-infusion in the first stages of brewing, to gain more equal extraction.
It is achieved by evenly wetting the ground coffee with a small amount of water (normally twice as much water in grams than the weight of the ground coffee), and letting them bloom for 20-30s before adding the rest of the water.

Once you have added the water, the coffee grounds expand and release the CO_2 created in the roasting process, this makes the coffee look like it is blooming, hence the name. The fresher the coffee, the bigger the bloom. Older or stale coffee beans don't have such a visual effect. This is because there is no or nearly no CO_2 left in the ground coffee, this means there is less resistance for the water and so the water passes straight through so doesn't create the 'bloom'.

Another way of blooming coffee than just adding water and letting it bloom is by using a spatula and quickly mixing up the coffee grounds with water. Ensuring that all grounds are wet (this is more often done when using a french press or an Aeropress)

Some might prefer one way of blooming to the other, but both of these approaches serve the same purpose.

Ideal set up for each brewing method

• Weigh your coffee beans and grind them just before brewing.
• If the brewing method requires a paper filter, rinse it with hot water.
• Place the brewer on the scale and add the grounds.
• Tare the scale.
• Brew, adding the water whilst keeping an eye on the scales, so that you know how much to add in order to maintain the correct ratio between ground coffee and water.

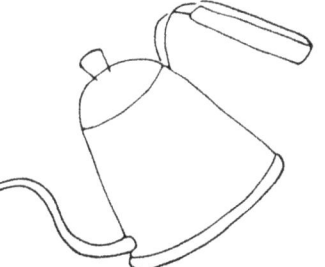

A kettle with a long swan neck is very handy as it allows you to pour water consistently, wetting all the grounds.

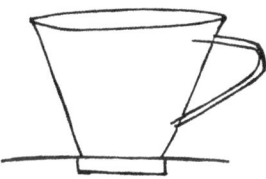

A digital scale is vital to maintain the right amounts of coffee and water.

Freshness of coffee
What is the big deal?!

The freshness of coffee is probably both its most important and its most overrated quality.
Coffee is organic matter. It doesn't stay the same forever; rather, it slowly goes stale (which can be noticeable in its taste).

This is true of all organic substances. The moisture content of green beans drops as the bean get older. The same thing happens with the aromatic gases produced when coffee beans are roasted. Therefore, the aromatic characteristics of coffee change over time, when the beans are harvested and roasted.

> Fresh coffee isn't necessarily nicer than older coffee, it is simply different.

The point of freshness and age of coffee suggests when the coffee will tastes its very best. This is specific to coffee, roasting manner and brewing method. A high concentration of gases is produced from the coffee beans during the roasting process. Roasted coffee beans are left to rest for approximately 4-7 days before they can be used for espresso preparations.
They are rested for 1-2 days for home brewing methods such as filters and the French Press.

> If the coffee has not been properly rested, it can taste overly acidic and harsh.

Ground coffee goes stale much faster than whole beans, especially if it is not stored in an airtight package. Coffee goes stale when the aromas evaporate off the bean. This causes the beans to become dry and lose their flavour.

The golden recipe for coffee

I have been looking for a golden recipe for years. A recipe that suits all coffee and brewing methods. How to prepare the best cappuccino, the ideal flat white, the perfect brew...However, I have come to realise that it just doesn't exist.

There is no golden recipe!

However, there are many interpretations of what is best and how to differentiate drinks from category to category (such as flat white, cappuccino and latte). There are also differing opinions on what makes a good brew and how the coffee beans should taste.

Different preferences and cultural traditions are what make coffee an enjoyable and exciting experience, which is why I am only suggesting a few guidelines to enable you to build your own golden recipe!

So go on, have fun, brew something and explore the variations! See how many different brews you can make using the same ingredients and altering the grind setting, water temperature and coffee to water ratio!

Chemex

Invented by German Scientist Dr. Peter Schlumbohm in 1941

Made of heat safe glass and a wooden collar for handling, this simple machine uses a pour-over/ filter coffee method and a paper filters that are much thicker than other filter papers, holding back more coffee solids and creating a lighter, smoother brew.

Perfect for serving 3-4 cups

Guidelines on how to brew
Start working out a recipe using
the following proportions:
33g of coffee
500g of water
Total brew time: around 5 min

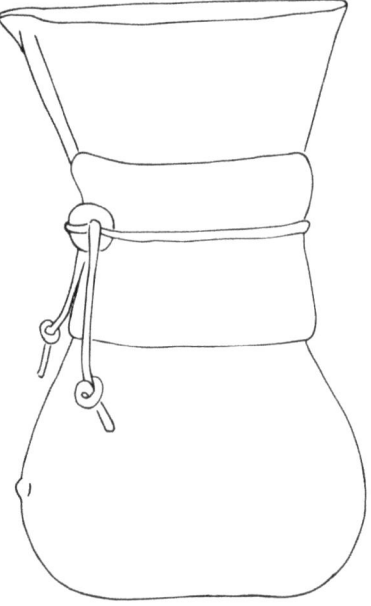

Place a 3 layered side of the filter against the spout. Pour some hot water through it first (to rinse it, make it sticky and preheat the surfaces).
Pour out the water, using the spout.
Place the ground coffee into the filter, and add 60g of water, and let it bloom for 25s.
Then keep topping it up with a smooth spiral pour of up to 500g of water.

Five min from when you added the first 60g of water, the brew should be ready.
Remove the filter containing the grounds, Swirl the Chemex to mix up the brewed coffee, and it's ready to be enjoyed.

Benjamin Jones

Benjamin Jones brewed coffee using a Chemex in the 2016 US National Brewers Cup competition. He points out to us the main advantages of using this brew method and has a couple of tips for a better result.

"2016 celebrated the 75th anniversary of the Chemex coffee brewer. I have been using one regularly for the last five years. I like the Chemex because it uses a very thick paper filter that pulls out most of the oils and fine coffee particles, leaving me with a cup that is light in body but emphasises the flavours of the brew.

The Chemex needs a moderate amount of care in brewing, but it is not a finicky brewer at all. I use 40-42 grams of coffee, ground between coarse drip and French press, and 700 grams of water. This will brew 2 mugs of coffee (appx. 590 mL). Total brew time falls between 4:00 and 4:30.

A few pointers:
Use the white filters and always rinse them before brewing.
I pour water in 3 stages: Slow bloom with 80g water, wait :30.
Bring water to 600g by 2:00. At 2:30-2:45, add the final 100g water."

Syphon

Invented by Loeff of Berlin in the 1830's but only became well known and used only after 1990's

The Syphon, or Vacuum pot, is one out of two kinds of brewers that use boiling water and don't require a kettle, as they have their own heating elements.

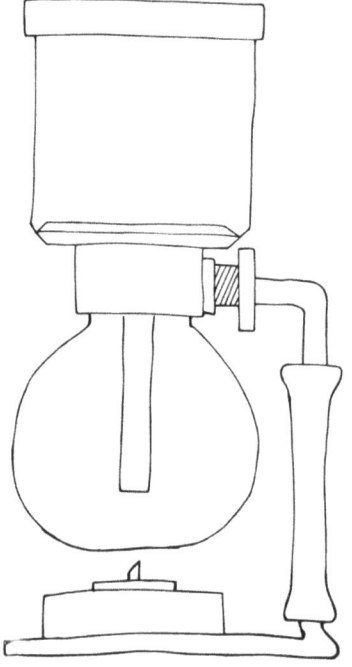

How it works: It has two bulbs connected to a tube, which holds a cloth filter. Underneath the lower bulb is a heating element that boils the water.

Pour water into the lower bulb. Assemble your Syphon, making sure that a filter is in place and hooked in. Add the ground coffee to the upper bulb. Light the burner and place it under the water bulb.

When the water starts to boil, it gets pushed up through the tube to the upper bulb. When all the water has gone through, start mixing the coffee grounds into the water, making sure that all the grounds are wet. After a minute, switch off the burner. This creates a vacuum in the lower chamber and causes the water to be sucked back down (and through the filter).
Now you have a filtered and very hot brewed coffee. Enjoy.

Before you start playing around with your syphon coffee brewer, I should warn you that it's hot hot HOT!

Regine won 2nd place at The World Syphonist Championship in 2016, representing Malaysia. As a Syphon master, she has a few tips to share about her approach to this complex brewing system.

Regine Wai Yee Beng

"Before I decided to participate in the Syphon competition, I knew nothing about it. It looks very elaborate. That's why to me, the Syphon makes the Syphonist look attractive and sophisticated.

But the more I learned about the Syphon, I fell in love with this brewing method, as it produces a consistent extraction yield and makes the coffee taste really fascinating. Unlike other brewing methods, the Syphon is basically brewing coffee at boiling temperatures, which means close attention is required.
Besides those factors, grind size and contact time are crucial to determine the flavour you would like to extract. Thus far, the Syphon remains my favourite coffee toy.

During the World Syphonist championship in 2016, I used a ratio of 1:11.11, ie 16g of coffee ground with 180g of water , a 50/50 blend of the Panama Ironman Geisha varietal (natural process) and the Costa Rica Dota El Diosa Geisha varietal (slow dried process).

I used a Fuji Royal grinder with a grind size of 3.5 (slightly fine), and I heated up for 45 sec. After numerous trials and practices, these are by far the best parameters that I found to be able to extract layers of flavours out of the blend.
As mentioned earlier, the Syphon requires close attention when brewing. You need to be quick in managing the brewing time and from overheating the brew. Once done brewing, you need to decide when to serve the coffee.

Serving your brew at the right temperature will determine what first flavours your customers will get, and more importantly, your brew won't burn your customers' tongues (remember, the Syphon brews at boiling temperature)."

Kalita

Kalita Wave- pour over brew method
This is a flat bottom filter that delivers amazingly consistent coffee cup after cup. The shape of the brewer has three perfectly positioned holes for dripping, which minimises the room for error. The only thing you need to be careful about is the filters. The filters are shaped in the form of a wave and can get easily damaged (which might cause the filter to get clogged and stop the water from passing through the holes).

Suggestions for use:

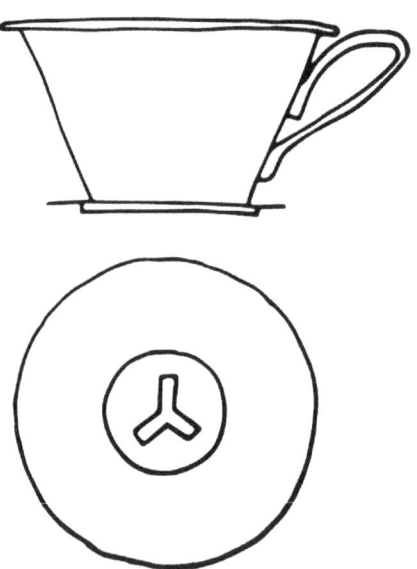

Rinse the filter with hot water. Distribute the coffee evenly. Add 40g of water and let it bloom for 25s. Keep adding more water in a slow, circular motion. Be sure to keep the level of water in the brewer to the middle (until you reach 308g of water).

Let it drip through. It might take between 4-5min from the beginning of the brew.

Carolina Franco de Souza

"As for many Brazilians coffee, has been an important part of my family for generations. Unfortunately, the coffee farm where my Great-grandfather built his dream was devastated by frost in the early 1960's and sadly, he passed away along with it.

Ever since, the family has had coffee in their hearts, but no one had the courage to build a life around it again. In 2002 my mother, Georgia Franco de Souza, decided to be brave again and open Lucca, the first specialty coffee roastery and café in Brazil. I was 10 when we opened, and the shop was my favourite playground. I loved to be around my mum and see what she was doing (I was very nosey).

Fortunately, she had the patience to teach me, and to this day she is my greatest hero. As the years passed, I started to source coffees from all over Brazil for Lucca and started helping to train our baristas at the café. Although after 14 years, I still can't steam milk properly, I can make a mean Kalita brew.

Kalita is a very versatile brew method. You can do so much with it, and it's very difficult to go wrong. The flat base will give you an even extraction, and the filter has a nice permeability that makes the coffee so clean.

When I won the Brazilian Brewers Cup championships in 2013 and 2015, Kalita was my first choice as a method for the coffees I had chosen. So here goes the recipe that got me 5th place on the World Brewers Cup Championship 2013 in Australia. I used a washed Brazilian coffee from Espirito Santo, but the recipe will work for most coffees, you just need to adjust the grind.

Recipe: 300g of water at 91C to 20g of coffee with a total brew time of 3:30min. Bloom the coffee for 30s. Next, pour water slowly over the ground coffee with circular movements for another 30s. Now straight pour for 30s and continue this until 300g of water has been added, and let it drip through."

V60

V60 Pour over method. 'V' refers to the shape of the machine, and 60 refers to the angle of the filter.

A very simple, fast and effective brewing method
Perfect for 1 or 2 servings

This device brews coffee similarly to the Chemex method. The only differences are the grind size and the filter paper. V60 brews are more bodied than those of the Chemex and are brighter than a brew with a Kalita Wave.

Brewing suggestion

Start with 15g of ground coffee
Add 30g of water
Let it bloom for 25s
With a smooth, circular pour, keep adding water until the amount reaches 230g in total.
Brew time is 2 - 2.30 mins.

Tetsu will now give us some tips about pouring water over the ground coffee to maximise brewing efficiency. His method won him the WBrC (World brewers cup championship) in 2016

Tetsu Kasuya

"For me, finding the easiest way to brew is the most important thing. I want to enable people to make coffee easily in their homes. It is weird for me that making coffee seems so difficult for coffee lovers (who are not professionals) and that they think only professionals can make coffee good.

I think that if everybody had the confidence that he can make coffee well, this wonderful industry would become more exciting and spread wider! My method is called the "4:6 method," which is the theme of my presentation for WBrC. It's very simple and easy to copy. You can make coffee like I do easily with this method.

First, divide the total water into 40% & 60% portions. Each portion has a different function. The 40% controls the balance between acidity & sweetness. The 60% is used only to adjust the strength of coffee. I pour the first 40% in 2 pours. If I use more water in the first pour, the acidity will be stronger. But if I pour less water in the first pour, the sweetness will be stronger. Now, the remaining 60% and the decision of how many pours remain. Usually I pour between 1 and 3 pours. If I use 3 pours, the strength will be stronger than if I use just 1 pour. So, the more pours you use, the stronger the coffee gets. In this "4:6 method", you begin each pour after all the liquid of the previous pour has dripped down into the decanter. This timing makes the extraction efficiency very high and also increases the strength of the brew for a coarsely ground coffee.

At WBrC, I used 20g of coarsely ground coffee and 300g of water whose temperature was 93 degrees. 40% of the 300g of water is 120g, and 60% is 180g. To emphasise the sweetness, I pour less in the first pour(50g) and 70g in the second pour. I aimed for a strong coffee, so I poured the 60% in three pours of 60g each. The timing for each pour was in 45second intervals, an ideal period of time for the water to drip down into the server. This method yields a coffee that is clean and sweet, with a long aftertaste. And the brewing is easy to copy, because the whole process is precisely measured.

This method is ideal for me, but no method is perfect, so please try it, share it so it can be loved and improved by everyone!".

Aeorobie- Aeropress

Invented by Alan Adler president of Aerobie Company in 2005
Widely used due to its simplicity.

Its an immersion coffee brewing method, in which the coffee is
infused in water and then forced through a paper filter with a
plunger)

Suggestions for use:

This brewer can be used in two positions:
traditional, and upside down (inverted
method). The brewing technique is the
same for either position.

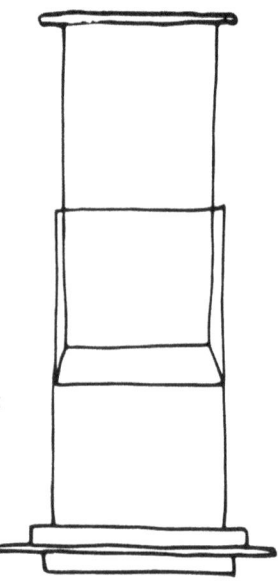

Inverted method.
Assemble the Aeropress and position it
with the plunger facing up.
Add 17g of ground coffee and 40g of water.
Stir it, making sure all the grounds are wet,
and leave it to bloom for 20s. Add the
remaining 180g of water and stir the brew a
couple of times.

Place a paper filter on the inside of the cup and rinse it with water.
Attach it to the Aeropress and let it sit for a minute. Then flip the
brewer over, place it over your mug, and push the plunger down.
The total brew time for this would be around 1:30 - 2 mins.

The traditional way to use the Aeropress would be to attach the
filter to the cup and place the brewer on top of the mug first. When
all the coffee grounds and water have been in contact for long
enough, insert the plunger into the tube and press down.

Lukáš Záhradník

"Lukas won the 2015 Aeropress Championship. His winning recipe was 20g of ground coffee to 260g of 80°C water, rewed just over 1.5 minutes. He has joined us to share his thoughts on the Aeropress and brewing.

The Aeropress is fast and easy and it eliminates mistakes. It is one of the things I use almost every day. It's light and flexible, so I can carry it whenever and wherever I go.

When I want a fast coffee, I always choose the Aeropress.
I like to play with my Aeropress most when I have an audience. Then, I like to try different grind sizes and different brew times, as these affect the taste of the cup!

My favourite recipe is very fast to make. If you have hot water it only takes 2 minutes to your first sip, but I prefer to wait longer and have my coffee cooled down. I think the Aeropress's main difference from alternative methods is the combination of full immersion coffee and drip coffee.

The Aeropress when used well, gives the cup more body and more juiciness. Once you have an Aeropress, you might become obsessed with its power.

My girlfriend Simona even uses coconut milk with a steel filter in her Aeropress. If you try it, you will definitely fall in love with this great toy. "

French Press

The French Press, or Cafetiere, or the plunger
Invented by the Italian designer Attilio Calimani in 1929

This brewer's infusion method uses a metal sieve to separate the grounds from the water. It is the easiest method of brewing. Here are a couple of tips for improving the brewing process.

Suggested recipe.

Place 20g of ground coffee and 40g of water into the Cafetiere, stir it and let it bloom. After 25s add 265g of water and put the plunger lid on. Leave it to infuse for a minute and then plunge it down.

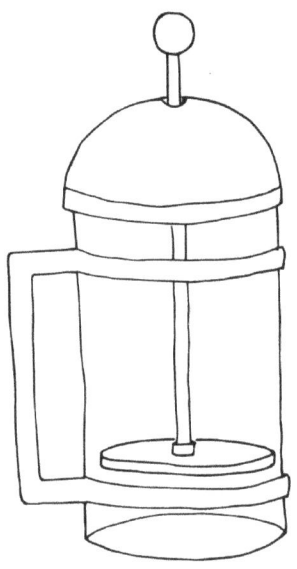

A tip here is to avoid letting the brewed coffee sit in the Cafetiere for long. This is because the water stays partially in contact with the coffee grounds, so the coffee will keep infusing, making it stronger and more bitter. To avoid this, simply pour any leftover brewed coffee into another server.

Rob used a French press when competing in the World Brewers cup in 2015. He used a very personal approach that changes the way the brewer itself was seen.

Rob Kerkhoff

"Before the Championships in Gothenburg of 2015, I began that year, with barista friends and colleagues, to experiment with brew methods.

I wanted to compete in the Brewers Cup. But I knew that two things in that competition were extremely important: consistency and taste. We threw everything that we already learned overboard and started all over again.

One brewer we liked was the Chemex. Not a catapult the brew method, but a paper filter. It yields such a beautiful, clean taste. But when searching for coffees during cupping, sometimes we found that the taste we achieved during cupping was better than the coffee that was brewed later. There were more deep flavours and aromas. After lots of experimenting we found that using an espro press and placing Chemex paper in between the microfilters worked awesome. With this you can combine the clean taste of a paper filter and the body and deep flavours of a cupping.

The espro press is the new French press. Better filtered with less grid. And by putting a paper filter in between the microfilter baskets, you have the best of two worlds. Infusion and pour over.

My recipe in the finals of Gothenburg was 15g coffee on 300 grams of water whose temperature was 93 degrees with 115ppm. I stirred 5,times, every 30 seconds, to keep the coffee in contact with the water. I pressed down at 4min, 30 seconds.

We discovered this way of brewing by experimenting and tasting. This method is not a holy grail, but I think it's a good starting point. You can use it to search for different methods, and hopefully thereafter you will share them with each other.

I also think that sharing knowledge and discoveries is the most fun part of the coffee community, and it helps bring the quality of speciality coffee to a higher level."

Clever Dripper

This machine is also called simply a Clever. It is the simplest brewer there is. It is an infusion brew method with a mechanical vent which, when opened after a brewing time, releases brewed coffee into a server through paper filter that separates it from any grounds.

It is not only simple to use but also delivers a very consistent brew.

A suggestion about how to use it

Place a paper filter into the brewer and rinse it with water. Empty the brewer and add 20g of coffee grounds and 40g of water. Let it bloom for 20s and then add 265g of water. Gently stir, then leave it to infuse for a minute.

Next, place the brewer on top of the mug or serving vessel. This frees the vent mechanism so that the brewed coffee flows through the filter into the vessel.
The result is a full-bodied and clear brew.

Anthony West

In 2011 the very first UK brewers cup was organised. Anthony West, Proprietor of the Black Chapel, took part in this competition, and he used a Clever drip brewer.

"Each competitor was given a time slot in which to produce three brews with competition-issued coffee and a competitor-chosen brew method. A brewer was defined as one that had no moving parts nor electrically produced water or some such. The idea was to use a gravity brewer, as up until this point, most competitive events had been centred around the World Barista Championship, which uses entirely espresso based coffee. I chose to use the Clever dripper, because it gives you complete control of brew time.

Going into a competition with an unknown coffee, I wanted to have the most versatile brew method. I used the generation one Clever dripper and Chemex papers that were folded flat. This would give a chewy feel to the coffee, no thinness. Using this set up was an attempt to cover all my bases. Brew fast and delicately if the coffee cups with acidic notes.

I dosed at 17.5g dry and 255g wet, hot water bloom, 25g (something I know now not to do as I used the Dagmar method of a cold water bloom). This brew method was geared towards bringing out the acidity in the cup, as I was using a washed heirloom coffee from Yirgacheffe, the Ethiopia Nordic style roast from Extract Coffee Roasters. Brewing with up to four minutes' immersion, the clever drippers hatch feature gave me so much control.

Unlike every other competitor I brewed my three cups in three brewers in parallel, as you would in a coffee shop, while they brewed in lots, barely scraping by to make the time. I clocked in under time by about 2 minutes and in the end I came 5th."

Moka

Invented in 1933 By the Luigi De Ponti (Italy) The Moka is also known as the Stove top.

This brewer uses a similar method to the Syphone. The lower chamber is filled with water, the middle of the brewer is filled with ground coffee, and the top part is for the brewed coffee. This method is different from the others in that the coffee is brewed with boiling water. When the brewer is filled with cold water and ground coffee and assembled, it is then placed on the stove or other heating element for brewing. For this reason, the Moka pot is known as a 'Stove top' as well.

When the water starts to boil, steam goes up through the tube into the upper chamber through the 'puck' of coffee grounds.

Here, the water and coffee grounds are in contact for a very short time (unlike in the Syphone method, where the grounds are steeped in water for a minute).
Because the Moka uses a metal filter, the brew is not as clear as it is in the methods that use a paper filter.

Suggestion for use:20g of ground coffee

Fill the lower chamber halfway with water.
Place the coffee in the filter basket and assemble the Moka pot.
Place it on a heating element. When the water starts to bubble, remove/switch off the heat. The steam will continue to go up through the coffee puck and your brew will be ready in seconds.
Flavour wise, Moka delivers a strong drink that resembles espresso.

GOAT STORY

GINA

"GINA: Smart coffee instrument is a novelty in the coffee market. It's a multifunctional coffee device designed by young Slovenian brand 'GOAT STORY'. GINA's main speciality is her multi-functionality. All of most manual coffee brewing techniques are now featured in one device. With specially designed valve, user can tune GINA and experiment with 3 different coffee brewing techniques within one coffee instrument. GINA users can choose classic pour-over, brew with immersion or try out cold drip technique.

Due to her versatility and simplicity, GINA is suitable for both first-time coffee brewers and experienced baristas.
She has a built-in Bluetooth scale that makes weighing the ingredients much easier, allowing the user to find the perfect ratio between coffee, water and time. Smart scale also connects with GINA app, which guides users through the whole brewing process towards the perfect coffee cup.

GINA is made to last. It's features are made of carefully selected materials: ceramic funnel with specially designed ridges for better coffee extraction, stainless steel frame for maximum stability, and borosilicate glass pitcher with small glass module for cold drip preparation. She is known for her sleek design: polished steel and powder coating finish in white, black or chrome.

TUNE THE TASTE WITH VALVE PRECISION

Leave the valve open for pour-over. Close for immersion or set the drop flow for drip. Leave the valve open for pour-over. Close for immersion or set the drop flow for drip. "

GOAT STORY
www.goat-story.com

"Meet the first coffee press that's as easy to use as it is easy to clean and is eco-friendly, too.
Our new manual brew method produces a sweet and balanced hand-crafted cup of coffee or tea. This is a unique new manual, single-serve coffee maker that combines the form of a French press with espresso-inspired technology to create a genuine new way to brew coffee or tea. By combining pressurized extraction with our patented reusable pod technology and ultra-fine 100 micron steel filtration, the American Press evenly extracts every ground of coffee to brew a clean, complex cup in less time with rich coffee oils preserved and less cup sediment than any other steel-filtered coffee maker.

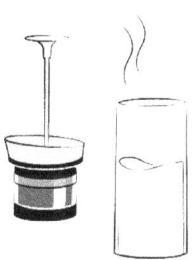

Put a little magic back in your mornings with an American Press coffee brewer
Just fill the pod with coffee (medium grind) add hot water, grasp the plunger assembly by the handle, then press the lid down to make sure it's fully seated.

Pre-infuse- most of the time we recommend pressing the pod down just enough to fill it with water (you'll see a little coffee emerging from the pod, which is your cue to stop pressing and start enjoying the sight of freshly ground coffee bubbling and foaming out of the pod as it off-gases, and the sight of your grounds expanding as they soak up water), and then wait anywhere from a few additional seconds to a couple minutes, depending on your own personal preference.
Press, and pour (without spilling a drop thanks to our carefully designed steel pouring edge). "

Alexander Albanese
Creator of American press
http://www.itsamericanpress.com

The Trinity ONE

"The Trinity ONE concept was dreamed up 3 years ago by founder, Mark Folker, who made his entry into specialty coffee coming from a background and interest in the specialty wine scene. After finalising his concept, Mark developed the design drawings for his new brewer, and then took it to Kickstarter where the project was funded.

Combining a number of popular brewing methods for specialty coffee – including press, drip and immersion brew methods – the Trinity ONE stirs up the traditional scene, and offers some additional brewing functionality that does not currently exist on other devices. The weighted cylinder offers self-pressing functionality which means consistent brewing that is unsurpassed on any other manual brewer. It is also presented in a stunning stainless steel and black walnut timber finish.

Mark said that the Trinity ONE allows a higher level of consistency and control when compared to other coffee makers on the market.
The Trinity ONE has been designed from day one to enhance the expression of the unique characteristics and regions of single origin coffee.

It is also modular in design, to allow the user to customise appearance and easily maintain. It is intended to last the long haul and will feature on any bench as a brewing appliance, not something to be hidden away. "

'Trinity Coffee Co'
Brisbane, Australia
www.trinitycoffee.co

The Phoenix

"The Phoenix is a minimalist approach to brewing coffee based on fundamentals of geometry, physics and chemistry. It is a framework to support a paper filter. The paper filter and the Phoenix together create the geometry of the brew column. The geometry of the brew column is a key element in the coffee brewing process. By changing the shape of the brew column you will alter the characteristics of the coffee that is brewed through it.

Depending on the type of the coffee being brewed, volume of desired output, and targeted cup profile there is a corresponding brew column shape that will optimize your success in brewing. – Patent Pending –

The Phoenix70 explained.
-Height Matters-

In an average 24 gram coffee brew with a standard 60 degree cone shape, the dry brew column is 2.25 inches tall. In an average 24 gram coffee brew with a 70 degree cone shape, the dry brew column is 3 inches tall. The 70 degree brew column is 33 percent taller, causing the brew water to travel further through the brew column. Therefore, by increasing the height of the brew column you are increasing the water to coffee contact. All else being constant, increasing the water to coffee contact results in more extraction of coffee solubles.

Secondly, the brew column serves as a filter. As the water moves through, coffee matter is carried downward. Most of the non-soluble matter is eventually trapped within the column, therefore acting as the primary filtering mechanism for the brew. The taller the brew column, the more non soluble coffee matter will stay in the brew column, resulting in higher cup clarity. In short, a taller brew column can help achieve higher extraction yields of coffee solubles and enhances cup clarity."

Khristian Bombeck
Saint Anthony Industries
www.stanthonyind.com

Cold Brew

More and more cold brewed coffee can be found in cafes and even in shop fridges. Cold brewed coffee is taking over iced coffees. which are Espresso served with cold milk over ice (with options of being stirred or shaken in cocktail shaker). You might ask, aren't iced coffee and cold brewed coffee the same thing? Not really. It's easy and fast to prepare an espresso shot and use it as a base for an iced coffee beverage, by topping up an espresso with cubes of ice, cold milk or water. But cold brewed coffee takes more time. Brewing time for this method can vary from 12-24 hours, depending on your recipe.

Cold brewed coffee is a relatively new thing and because it is new, it is unclear what factors affect the cold brew process. However, there are a few methods that the coffee be brewed.

Cold brewed coffee uses cold water for a long coffee infusion. Using cold water makes the coffee extraction very slow and gives the coffee a different taste from the hot brew methods. Cold brewed coffee has more consistent flavours over time and can be stored in the fridge for up to a week. This is because less oil is extracted from the coffee.

A cold brewed coffee beverage like this has no preservatives, so storing it increases the possibility of bacteria. The chance of bacteria is increased if sugar is added, as this gives the bacteria energy to grow.

A simple method of preparing this beverage uses a French Press with a ratio of 100g of coffee to 1 litre of water.
The coffee needs to be ground to a size suitable for French Press, since the difference in method is that you pour over cold water instead of hot!

Then, place the French Press into the fridge to infuse for 12-24hrs. Once the coffee is ready, simply plunge the French Press to separate the grounds from the brewed coffee. For a clearer brew, you can filter it through filter paper, in order to get rid of small bits of coffee). Your freshly brewed coffee is now ready to be enjoyed!

Stempels' Slowbrew

"There is no certainty of how coffee will turn out without experimentation and adopting to each different coffees individual type. A couple of innovative brothers have come up with an idea. The discovered how to cold brew coffee at its best and also the best way to bottle it and keep it fresh for selling.

The two brothers Jan and Niclas Stemplewski came across the completely new interpretation of coffee that is Cold Drip while road-tripping through Australia. Sipping their first Cold Drip Coffee the two founders of Slowbrew Cold Drip Coffee realised how complex coffee actually is. The coffee fruit has much more to offer than the roasted flavour usually associated with it.

Like wine or whiskey, coffee can offer quite different notes: fruity, floral, spicy or smoky. For the brothers, the Cold Drip method is the perfect way to gently extract these different flavours from the coffee beans. That is why they spent countless hours in order to develop their own production device. The production device a.k.a „The Beast" is based on the cold drip method, of which they thought to receive the most delicate results in cold extraction. Within five to seven hours of extraction, depending on the recipe, they highlight the specific natural aromas of each coffee they use without the usual deviation in taste by temperature, pressure or organic filter materials. The results range from beautiful nutty and cacoa to ice tea like and very fruity or even wine and whiskey like flavours. Fitted to the aromatic characteristics they treat the cold drip to endure a shelf live of 6 weeks up to 6 month, without loosing its delicate flavours.

Slowbrew is brewed, bottled and labeled by hand with great attention to detail. The brothers use coffee from small roasters, which buy their beans directly from the coffee farmers. This way Slowbrew guarantees high quality and producers receive their fair share also #brewloveistruelove"

Jan and Niclas Stemplewski
http://www.slowbrew.de

At your cafe

As I mentioned before... The days when a cup of coffee was just a coffee are long gone... and it can be quite confusing looking at a coffee menu nowadays! This is without even thinking about all the names for cup size options which are used in different places! Have no fear! I will give you a guide to the modern menu to help you find the drink you fancy!

At a regular cafe, all coffee drinks (apart from filter coffees) are espresso-based. However, there is a coffee that is a mix of filter and espresso...It is called a 'red eye' or 'black eye' depending on the number of espresso shots added to the filter coffee.

The espresso based drink that falls into the category of "black coffee," or regular coffee, is the Americano or Long black or Espresso.

Long Black- Espresso with a dash of hot water.
Americano- Espresso with nearly a full cup of hot water.

Everything else espresso based on the menu is an espresso topped with milk.

Macchiato – An espresso-sized cup with hot milk (ratio of 2:1), or it could also be an espresso topped with spoonful of milk foam.

Flat white – Usually served in a standard size cup. It is a double espresso (or ristretto) with flat milk (milk that is not very foamy). The focus of a flat white is the strong flavour of the cup--this drink highlights the characteristics of the coffee.

Latte – Usually served in a larger cup or with a smaller amount of espresso than the other drinks. A latte is filled with lots of steamed milk and makes a light milky coffee.

Cappuccino – Can be served with either a double or single espresso shot. It is made with sweet foamy milk. The balance between coffee and milk demonstrates a nice contrast between the highlighted coffee characteristics and the sweet milk.

Coffee with milk

There are no golden recipes for drink preparations. Nor are there universal standards for how each drink should be presented and differentiated from another drink (especially milky drinks like the Cappuccino, Latte and Flat White)
All good cafes interpret their beverages in their own way, doing the best that they can.

However, some cafes do not try and differentiate between these drinks at all. Instead of naming the coffee on the menu, they present it as coffee with steamed milk, only giving cup size options that vary the ratio of espresso and milk.

Brazil as a cappuccino please

Some cafes don't stick to one coffee origin or blend but rather have many different coffee origins and blends to offer, which can be prepared in many different ways.
This is a great way to introduce coffee origins to customers, so that they can discover diverse flavours, especially if they can purchase the beans afterwards to take home.

What you see on these menus are the coffee producing countries or names of the farms, followed by methods of how the coffee can be brewed.

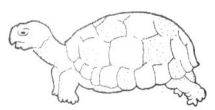

Sizes
Does size matter?

The truth about different sized coffee options are that they are rarely consistent in proportion.

Quite often, the drink the next size up is just topped up with extra milk or water. This creates a more diluted and weaker-flavoured cup. Using the same amount of coffee for all sizes is a very common thing for cafes to do. If a cafe were to give a single shot in one size and a double shot of espresso in the next size up, with the aim of consistency in flavour, then the next size up would have to be twice as large.
However in most cafes, the next size up is normally only 2 to 4 oz. larger, so adding an extra shot of espresso doesn't make sense.

This is the reason why some places do not offer size options. Making different types of coffee is like making cocktails...

It is all about making sure each part of the drink is in the right proportion to the other parts, in order to bring out the best possible flavour.

Our perspective of coffee

Accompanying a rise in cafes around the world that proudly serve high quality coffee, is a rise in baristas who take pride in preparing it to reach its best taste. Their practices vary from place to place, but the focus remains the same: coffee that perfectly embraces its characteristics. Baristas like these are true artisans, masters of their crafts.

Traditional cafes, which mostly use coffee blends of Arabica and Robusta beans (see page 5) take pride in what they do, holding onto longtime expectations for the taste of their coffees.

Other places that go by the name 'cafe' might be very far in approach from the artisanal cafes, although their menus might read the same. Their approaches to delivery of the coffee can be very poor, which can leave us with the misperception that coffee is just a bitter morning kick.

Synthetic-flavoured coffee cocktails are usually on display in places like this.

These again are very far from anything that can be called coffee. Coffee cocktails are made of espresso topped up with loads of milk, spiced up with sugary, synthetic flavour syrups and served with a yet more sugary dollop of whipped cream.

Coffee is great in its pure form: its simplicity and complexity needs no preservatives. If it drowns in other flavours, it is no longer a simple coffee anymore, it is a cocktail.

"Coffee is a language in itself."

–Jackie Chan

Misconceptions

Some misconceptions about the quality of coffee, and what makes a well prepared brew.

Crema which holds sugar

It is thought that you can identify the quality of an espresso by its thick, rich crema, and that this is tested by how quickly sugar falls through the top (the slower the better). However, this is a misconception. The thickness of the crema does not say anything about the quality of coffee.

But its colour and texture says a lot about how well it has been prepared. Ideally it should be smooth, with no white dots but some lines across it's surface.
*Crema- The golden brown layer that covers the surface of an espresso.

Hot Coffee

It is a misconception that espresso-based coffees (such as cappuccino and latte) should be served hot. These beverages were designed for immediate consumption, so they shouldn't be served boiling hot, as you might expect. For more about beverage temperature, see page 65

Strong coffee

A coffee bean, by itself, is not any stronger or weaker, in a general sense, than other coffee beans. Beans can have differing percentages of caffeine, they can have different qualities such as more body or acidity... but none of these qualities affect the strength of the coffee.

Strength is a term that used to describe how a coffee is brewed. Strength is not associated with the coffee bean of origin. How strong a coffee is comes down to how it is brewed - The same coffee can be brewed stronger or weaker, depending on what you want. Some coffee beans are more soluble than others. The degree of the roast (how darkly roasted the coffee is) can also affect coffee solubility. This can make the process of producing a stronger brew faster.

If your brewed coffee tastes too strong, it can be diluted with extra hot water or milk. To make a stronger coffee, a finer grind setting should be used, to increase the amount of contact time the coffee grounds have with the water. Another way of making a stronger coffee is using less water for the same amount of ground coffee.

"Have loads of coffee and have most productive day what world have seen."

-Luke Tariq Lamb

Barista Routine
Espresso and milk

The Barista's main responsibility is to bring out the best from the coffee and the milk. They do this by mixing them up in perfect harmony, and a good barista delivers a great experience to the customer.

Most of the conditions that are needed for delivering one good espresso after another are pre-set. The dose of coffee is one of these conditions.

With the simple touch of a button on an espresso machine, a pre-set amount of water goes through the coffee.

Then, the coffee extraction depends on how long it takes for the water to pass through the ground coffee.

The most important skill is taste, and a barista will always make changes in the recipe or extraction time based on how the coffee actually tastes.

As we already know, in coffee preparation, several parameters affect the taste of the brew, so attention to detail is necessary to deliver the same product consistently throughout the day.

The time period of the extraction is the only part of the espresso recipe that is not constant. It can change according to the time of the day or how busy the cafe is.

The barista changes the parameters by altering the grind setting on the machine several times during a day.

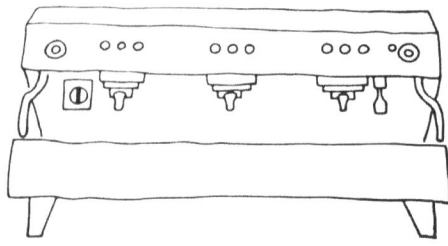

Preparing an espresso

•Clean the filter basket and ensure that it is completely dry.

•Fill the basket with the desired dose of coffee.

•Distribute the coffee grounds evenly in the filter basket.

•Tamp the coffee down.

•Clean the edges of the filter basket.

•Insert a porta-filter into the group head* and immediately press the button to start the water flowing. (*Group head-part of the espresso machine to which the porta-filter is attached)

The key factors here are:

•A clean, dry porta-filter avoids channeling of the coffee . If there is any moisture left in the basket before the ground coffee is added, then the water for extracting the coffee might not go through the coffee puck but rather pass over the sides of the filter, barely touching the coffee grounds. Water is lazy, it likes to the find easiest route.

•An even distribution of coffee grounds in the basket is important for an even extraction. Similarly to the channeling situation, the water will not flow through the coffee puck evenly if there is not even distribution, causing one side of the coffee puck to be barely touched by water. This is more noticeable when you use a double-shot porta-filter, because the espresso will not flow evenly from both spouts.

•Tamping is not complicated at all. It is just pressing and compacting the coffee grounds tighter together. The hard part of tamping is applying consistent pressure each time. Mistakes in tamping, such as over-tamping or under-tamping, become apparent in the period of extraction. If it takes longer for water to pass through the coffee puck, then too much pressure has been applied in tamping. It is over-tamped. If the extraction time is too fast, then the coffee has been under-tamped and not enough pressure was used.

•Cleaning the sides of the basket is important for the espresso machine and will make the rubber seals that are inside of the group head last longer.

Coffee tampers can be found in various designs, weights and sizes. A tamper base – the part which is in contact with the coffee grounds (coffee puck) can vary from flat to convex (slightly angled so that the middle is deeper than its edges). The tamper base shape changes the way the water flows through the puck.

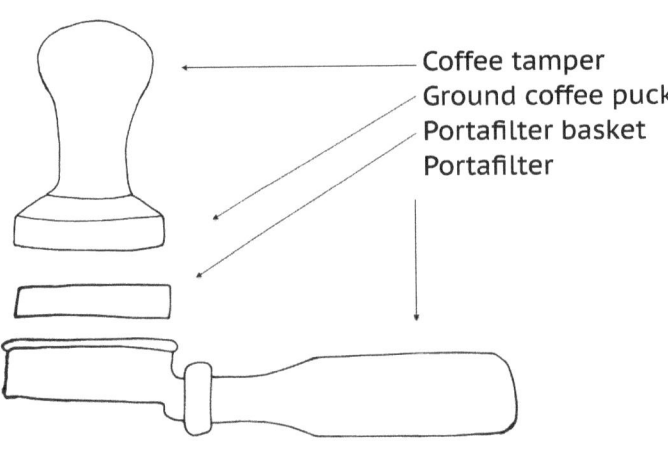

Coffee tamper
Ground coffee puck
Portafilter basket
Portafilter

Even though tamping is not complicated at all, there is a lot of room for error, due to all the aspects of tamping and how it can affect extraction, therefore taste.

To make ground coffee tamping easier and to ensure consistency in tamping shot after shot, the 'Clock Work Espresso' Company came up with a design that takes away the possibility of over or under tamping during a busy day at a cafe.
See what they have to say about it on the next page.

CLOCKWORK ESPRESSO

"PUSH is an adjustable tamper, which allows the user to set the depth based on their recipe, lock it in, and then reproduce identical and perfectly level tamps every time, for every user. It was used by Maxwell Colonna-Dashwood (UK champion) in the 2015 World Barista Championships, in Seattle, and is now regularly used in competitions around the world.

When making espresso, the pressurised water will find the path of least resistance through the compressed bed of coffee grounds. If tamped correctly, the entire puck should resist the flow of water equally, causing the water to flow evenly through the grounds, and so evenly extracting the soluble compounds in the coffee.

If the grounds are not tamped correctly, the water will rush through wherever it can, resulting in under extracted espresso.

PUSH has also been found to significantly reduce the risk of injury to baristas, when compared with a traditional tamper. Baristas commonly suffer from injuries from tamping coffee, but the neutral posture which PUSH allows them to use is a welcome relief for many."

Pete Southern
Clockwork Espresso
www.clockworkespresso.com

Preparing the steamed milk

Milk steaming is very simple.

•Pour cold milk into a clean, dry pitcher until it is 1/3 full.

•Insert the steam arm a few millimetres into the milk and point the tip of the arm to 3 o'clock.

•Open the steam tap. As soon as the steam starts to flow, the milk will whirl around in the cup .

•Lower the jug by half a centimetre. Lowering the jug by this small amount makes the milk more aerated, so it will create more foam.

•Keep the pitcher in the same position until the milk reaches the required temperature. Normally 150-160F is the temperature at which milk tastes sweetest. If milk gets hotter than this, the sweetness, texture and flavour of the milk are less pleasant.

The key factors here are as follows:
Always use cold milk and a clean pitcher for best results.
Create the foam as you open the steam tap. The more time you let the milk spin in the jug, the glossier it will get.
If you aerate the milk too late (when it is nearly up to temperature), there won't be enough time to smoothen the milk and get rid of all the bubbles (by letting it spin). This will result in too much foam, which is not appealing to see.
A perfectly steamed milk should look like glossy wet paint and will have no bubbles present. It will taste sweet and have a nice texture.

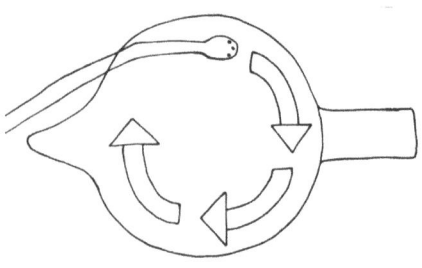

Going in deeper

Classes and lectures are not only for beginners, they are for anyone keen to go into more depth, and gain a full understanding of coffee. They are a chance to fill in knowledge gaps and give students of coffee an opportunity to ask questions.

The purpose of learning, after all, is to discover how little we know. And coffee can be a great new topic to learn about.

The first classes I took completely changed the way I approached coffee and set me on a path of constant learning and improvement.

Places like the Espresso Academy in Florence provide all kinds of barista training and coffee workshops. They are always expanding, offering a wide range of classes and a frequently updated blog, so you can follow their activities and posts about coffee. Their website is a great way to stay updated on and connected to the world of coffee.

Mokaflor- Espresso Academy

"Everything started in 2009, when Gabriele Cortopassi created the blog ilcaffeespressoitaliano.com (The Italian espresso) in order to present to the world a modern approach to coffee in Italy and in Italian. The blog grew out of the site aprireunbar.com (open a bar), which launched earlier and resulted in a book of the same name.

Due to the high demand at his roasting company and various other commitments, Gabriele eventually couldn't continue updating the blog, and in 2012, Simone started collaborating with him. They met in a coffee course at the academy that at the time was only for Mokaflor customers. The blog now has reached 35000 visits per month and sparkles with fresh posts every day, featuring news from international coffee exhibitions and experiments being performed in the school. It has become a useful handbook for many Italian baristas wanting to know more about their passion.

Now, the school (Espresso Academy) offers courses both for Italians and for international students. Among baristas around the world, there have long been knowledge gaps, and the school was created in order to fill them in and immerse a student, at a professional level, in the basics of coffee tasting, latte art, roasting, barista skills and brewing. For some people, it's a new world, and once you are into it, it's difficult not to go deeper.

A lot of passion and time have been the keys to the project's success. The school was born out of need and it has become a pleasure to watch students fulfill their dreams."

Founders and trainers of Espresso Academy
Simone Celli and Gabriele Cortopassi

For more details about classes email at
corsi@aprireunbar.com

Espresso Academy Firenze
www.aprireunbar.com

- Espresso Academy -

Firenze

Coffee has more to offer than only a bean

The cascara or cherry pulp of a coffee bean is the sweet fruity part that holds all the sugars. When dried, it retains its sweetness and flavour. This dried fruit can create great infusions, making a Cascara tea.

A friend, who works on researching all aspects of Cascara also works with farmers to supply it wholesale, along with regular green coffee beans. Below is some knowledge of cascara and his research work.

"The development of Cascara as an ingredient in beverages and foods has so many benefits. It contributes to sustainability, as a former waste product converted into a consumer product; it provides additional financial benefits to the farmer, by providing a new revenue stream; and it provides nutritional benefits to the consumer as cascara is high in fibre, protein, carbohydrate, vitamin and antioxidant content and can be considered a superfood.

But producing good cascara is not an easy task, and it takes careful attention in processing in order to produce a product with all the flavour and sweetness that consumers demand that is also free from contamination, particularly pesticides and mycotoxins.

Each variety, like roasted coffee, has a unique flavour and nutritional characteristics. In fact, we are finding differences in nutritional characteristics between growing regions as well. Cascara, like roasted coffee, provides a rich research opportunity, and its full nutritional profile and potential health benefits are not yet understood.

 I expect many years of interesting information to come from the research being conducted and expect that entrepreneurs will continue to create many interesting products as well".

Joel Jelderks

And here we have reached the end of our introduction to coffee in this textbook. I think there is no way to overstate how complex the journey is from bean to cup.

The dedication that people in the coffee industry have for their beloved product is truly amazing. The price we pay for coffee is just a small piece of gratitude for all their hard work.

I hope that you have found these pages interesting to read and that they will come in handy as you explore the world of coffee! Remember to share your coffee experience and prepare some unforgettable brews, because coffee is the best excuse to sit down and have a chat.

For me, this little book has been a massive learning process and a chance to connect with some amazing, likeminded people. This book has helped me to rediscover how diverse the coffee world is.

The number of people passionate about coffee is definitely what amazes me the most.

Thank you.

THE
END

Credits

Text Editor / Ghostwriter - Emily Carroll

Ilustrations - Niamh Laurie Proctor
pages: 4;10;55;56;57

References

Websites:
www.Coffeeimports.com
www.ncausa.org

Books:
'Coffee' by Cladia Roden
'The coffee roasters companion' by Scott Rao

Inspitarions
Movies:
'Film about coffee' 2014
'Barista' 2015

Notes

Lightning Source UK Ltd.
Milton Keynes UK
UKHW030752240419

341527UK00013B/1026/P